Life Skills &
College Planning
Made Easy:

Everything a Teen Needs to Know

A Book For Teens, Young Adults and Parents.

How to plan for college, look for scholarships, and where to begin. Equip yourself with knowledge.

Patrice Torrez

Written By: Patrice Torrez ©
Cover by Hector Curriel ©Patrice Torrez 2017
2017 ISBN: 978-0-9993771-0-9

First Edition: May 2017

This book was written to teens, for teens, parents and guardians by the parent of a teen who once was a teen looking at the prospect of college. It's the book I wish I had for the younger me.

Table of Contents

I spent the first six months of my student's senior year planning and preparing her for college. My plan was to be more than ¾ of the way done by mid school year. In order to reach that goal, I started reflecting on everything I'd done since ninth grade to prepare her for college. For example, the first week of ninth grade year, I found 11 schools, some of which she had mentioned and some she had not. I went online and requested information about the school and the chosen major at the time. I had to call some of the schools to request information, while some I requested online. They all sent information via snail mail for her to review which she gladly did. I knew that I did not want my children to have a ton of debt during and just after college. It's really tough when you graduate with a mountain of debt before you even have time to find a job. I've been there, I've done it, and wrote this book about it to help you not do it.

Unnecessary debt can potentially be setting you up for failure. That's not to say that education debt is an absolutely no no. I'm moreless stating that you have to use wisdom when acquiring debt. There are some instances that it can not be avoided if you want to attend college and make a better life for yourself. That's when planning and educating yourself comes in hand.

Working in the field of education for so long really helped me to gain valuable information and a greater understanding for things related to secondary and postsecondary education and debt. It's something that I did not want for my children, so I planned early and found resources to eliminate the necessity for debt as much as possible.

Accumulating debt for college may be unavoidable for some. That does not mean that you can't find ways to either eliminate or minimize the amount of debt you incur. As long as you have the ability to try, you can help steer your own path. If you're a senior and you're starting to think about planning, get started right now. If you're a freshman in high school, it's not too early to plan. There's a whole chapter designed to guide you through preparing for college from ninth through twelfth grade. Wherever you are in this process, start planning. Just because you're late to this party, doesn't mean you don't show up. You may be fashionably late to my post secondary planning party, but it doesn't mean you're going to miss out on all the fun. I've been to college, earned a few degrees along the way and even in writing this book, I gained more knowledge- so it's never too late to learn. One of the secrets to gaining wisdom is understanding that you are never too old to learn, so prepare yourself for what's to come.

I began journaling in an effort to organize my plan. I created a list of items to buy, things to do, etc. This book started off as a journal of my adventures in helping my child prepare for her college experience. It quickly turned into a journal about helping my child become an independent adult because of course that was important as well. I wanted to replay all the lessons and teachable moments in my head to see if I had in fact done what I set out to do- teach her how to adult, how to be responsible, how to learn from her mistakes . I wanted to make certain she was prepared. That's when I realized that my teen wasn't the only one who may need guidance in preparing for college and independent living. I realized that others more than likely needed that same thing.

I doubt I am the only person who has asked themselves if they've done their job as a parent. Have I taught them the things they need to know? How to think independently, to have integrity, how to be a leader so they know where they are going and not be lead nowhere, and all the other things you wonder. It is a lot to remember over the years. My hope is that this book will be a guide in preparing for college and by the time you reach the end, you will have learned a lot and are steps closer to being college ready. Please read from cover to cover to gain the most value.

Thank you so much for your reading this book.

INTRODUCTION

If you are reading this book, chances are you are curious about what you need to do to become college ready. Sure, they tell you the basics right? They tell you to go to school, get good grades, take the tests and apply to colleges. They tell you to stay focused and to graduate. Right? What they don't tell you is why or how to do most of it. Many people are advised to start the process in eleventh grade, but to keep your grades up throughout high school. The truth is that there is so much more you can do if you start early that could potentially reward your hard work and effort. The trouble is, you're usually not privy to this information.

That's where this book comes into play. Some counselors are great. They share what they know, how it works, etc. Some will tell you to the take the ACT or SAT whenever you want if it is before 11th grade whereas some will advise against it. In many instances, there are phenomenal counselors and teachers. My very own student had probably the best counselor hands down. I can't honestly even recall my high school counselor's name. I don't remember him or her. My experience with my student's high schoolers counselor was actually quite the opposite. If any counselor was more giving of his or her time, I would be amazed. My student's counselor was knowledgeable, encouraging, forthright and had the perfect balance of accountability. I witnessed it on several occasions not just with my student, but with others as well. It did not matter the student, she always brought her A game. She gave us great, insightful information and I took what she gave and expanded on it. She sent us down a path that led us to sweet victory. It was a culmination of the counselor giving me the bread crumbs to start researching and my pre-planning the moment my high schooler became a high schooler that yielded us the results we desired.

We oftentimes hear these stories of students earning six figure scholarships and having choices to attend many universities. It's tougher to get into colleges and universities nowadays because it is more competitive. Not only that, it's expensive as well and most college students graduate with some form of debt. Living in the age of technology, you have access to things others who came before you did not. Information is literally at your fingertips. I remember reading a story of a young girl who banked a whopping $80,000 dollars in scholarships to pay for college. Another student earned over one million dollars in scholarships- enough to pay for college through his PhD program. He won 35 scholarships in total. Both students had to step outside of the norm to make this happen. They had to be diligent and work hard to make it happen. They also made earning the grades their priority. They did the research, the work and the essays and the end result was beneficial for them. Now, will it happen to every student? Probably not because it takes a lot of effort, but do the work and see what type of results you produce.

It is important to be wise and do your research, so that you pick reputable websites before you apply and provide your personal information. With that being said, there are sites out there designed specifically for you to earn college scholarship money. That's right, you can actually bank scholarship money to pay for college. Continue reading this book to help you become more prepared for college living-after all, there is more than just scholarships to consider.

Let me ask you a question...

Even as a teen, would you go back in time and tell the younger you not to do something or to do something differently? Who wouldn't right? From the smallest of things to something you'd rather not think about. We've all done something that we aren't proud of or that we look back on and think it was just ridiculous. It could have been something so silly as a temper tantrum over a toy you didn't get that you really don't care two flips about now. My point is this- you can learn from your mistakes. If adults are genuinely looking out for your best interest giving you advice that might actually help you, why wouldn't you listen? Do you take the time to weigh the validity of the information or do you automatically discard it?

Here's the thing. You have some people who take the information and discard it as soon as it given because they've deemed the source unreliable. "It's just my mom or just my dad. They have to say those things because they love me," or my favorite, "It's not like it was when you were young." Well, that's partially true, but honestly the more things change, the more they remain the same. The world is changing in many ways, but there's nothing new under the sun. The truth is we were all young at some point and probably thought the same way some of you do, but then we grow and realize that hey, maybe they are giving me sound advice because maybe they experienced something similar. Half the things going on in the world were not invented by your generation. We're not talking about actual inventions here, we're talking about how your parents were young once upon a time and know a thing or two regardless of whether or not you give them credit for it.

It's like this... if your parents are telling you that maybe there are scholarships out there for certain things, maybe there actually are scholarships out there. If you don't apply, I guarantee you that someone else will. I can also say that beyond a shadow of a doubt you that if you don't apply, you will not get the scholarships you didn't apply for. You will eliminate every possible chance of earning any scholarships if you don't apply because you think it's a thing of the past- as if it doesn't exist anymore. The choice is yours. You can either research and apply for what you might qualify for or you can be one of those who believe already that they are not going to win any scholarships, so they don't apply. Those are the ones who essentially have talked themselves out of the money and therefore forfeit their chances. I'm not suggesting you apply for everything, I am however suggesting that you apply, apply, apply! When you feel like you're done and don't want to apply for more, but there's still more scholarships available, apply some more! You don't know which ones you will actually earn. This is why you need to apply to as many as there are available.

Research and apply because many students will not take the time to write an essay or two. Recycle essays whenever possible, change them to match the criteria for the scholarship, but use the foundation of what you've created. Work smarter in the situation and use the harder part for maintaining stellar grades. Did you know that many students think they don't qualify for scholarships or that they don't exist, so they don't apply? Those same students miss out on so much just because they made an incorrect assumption. Again, research is the key here. You have to research to determine the legitimacy of the scholarships. This where you enlist the help of your parents, guardians, loved ones or a high school counselor. Find someone who knows or is happy to work with you and to find out.

Fact: You will be doing a lot of research on your own. You just have to determine whether or not it's worth it to you.

CHAPTER 1
Basic life skills

Life skills are essential to being a productive citizen. These are skills needed, acquired or desired to manage your life. As a parent/ guardian, most of us find every opportunity to make something into a teaching moment. We don't necessarily look for them, but they are ever present and plentiful. How many eye rolling moments did you have after experiencing a teachable moment, then later realize you were glad you learned it? Often times, as parents/ guardians, we conceal our emotions so that the message is actually heard and received. Meanwhile in our heads we are singing a celebratory tune when our child says something or does something to be proud in response. They just don't always let you know it for fear it would diminish the message, but it's a proud moment indeed.

Through the years, I have used family/quality time to teach life skill lessons like cooking, baking, sewing, etc. For example, my daughter and I years ago made pillows and clothes for her dolls. I did it for the fun in it and the quality time, but it just so happened to teach her a life skill- she learned how to sew. It may sound a little familiar or maybe completely bizarre to you, but we have family meetings where we discuss and create budgets, vision boards, and goal sheets with action plans. This too serves dual purposes. We work as a family to set goals. It teaches them to set SMART goals that are specific, measurable, attainable, realistic and timely and at the same time allows them to put a plan in motion. It's not fair to just have the kids do this or for the adults to just do it. The truth is, most all of us have dreams and goals. Why wouldn't we get a head start on how to work towards making them a reality?

Four years of high school will go a lot quicker than you can imagine. Each person reading this book is at a different stage/grade and preparation level. If you've experienced similar things, learn to appreciate the effort and realize that it will help you now that college is in the near future. If you haven't there's no better time than now to sit down with your parents/guardians or friends and have fun learning some of these things. If this is a completely different concept to you or your family or friends, research online how to do this. Remember that in the age of technology, you can easily learn about cooking, sewing, money, etc. There are so many diy (do it yourself) videos out there. When I don't know how to do something, I search online and find how to videos and instructions. What I've learned is that people are often times eager to share what they know. There are also community enrichment classes in most cities that offer a variety of classes at reasonable prices. I am by definition a bargain shopper. Use your resources and find good deals if you are looking for classes, otherwise look online. Having a friend or family member take a class with you only adds to the fun.

While most people associate life skills with how to do this that and the other (and they are associated with those things), they are also general things like your moral compass, your beliefs, how you treat people and material things (yours and other people's belongings), how you handle situations, etc.- essentially how to do this thing called life. It is a small title that encompasses so much.

Often times, we get to senior year and we start looking back at how quickly time has flown by. We wonder if we've done everything we could have to prepare our children for adulthood. Do you feel like you're ready for the next step in life? What do you already know how to do? What do you want to learn how to do? Have you tried it or is it just a hunch? Try cooking. Go shopping with your parents or guardians and help them shop. See what it's like to shop and stick to a budget. This is the perfect opportunity to see how it's done before it's thrust upon you with little or no knowledge. If you have budget conscious parents or guardians, now you will realize why you don't get every single thing you requested from the grocery. After you've gone grocery shopping, come home and help cook. Why stop there? Volunteer to cook once a week or month.

If this is something you already do, then kudos to you. If not, give it a try. Perfect a few signature dishes, then add to your repertoire. You will be cooking more than one dish in no time.

Basic life skills are essential to helping students transition from high school to college living and into young adulthood. At times, I felt bad for my kids because I was an educator. That literally meant that I was constantly teaching my kids something. It wasn't always school subjects. Sometimes it was how to cook or bake or how to separate clothes. Sometimes it was school related things. In the not too distant past, my youngest came home with an assignment in social studies. He had questions for me about what he was reading. I knew some of the answers and some I did not. Since we live in this lovely era of modern day technology, it was easy to research the answers. The typical person would have stopped there, but we were both intrigued so we watched a documentary about it. My child was so excited to learn more than what the assignment called for. As the suspense built in finding these truths, we were both conversing on our speculative answers. We didn't stop there. We watched another documentary on something closely related over the course of the next few days, then we talked about what we learned. I didn't trick him into learning, we just had fun while learning. Not everything you learn is fun, but when it is it's just better all around. Not only did he learn more about the subject, but also how to research when you don't know the answer.

I wish I had composed a list over the years of things I set out to teach my children a lot sooner. The list below is a list of things that I personally have made a point to teach my kids along with a list of items from parenting.com, livingwellspendingless.com and good old fashion experience. Here are things you need to learn or evaluate:

1. Values/ Principles, Beliefs and how to come to their own conclusions.

2. Hygiene- Take care of you mind, body and soul. (Learn how to cook. Ask a parent or guardian to teach you, ask if you can take classes or go online and watch videos. Learning to navigate in the kitchen isn't a gender specific thing. Take care of yourself and maintain a healthy lifestyle)

3. Self discipline- Learning when and how it applies to you. (i.e. How not to spend your last dime, how to wait and not be impulsive, when the first piece of cake is enough, to eliminate procrastination, eat healthy, study early, follow up on important things, set priorities for yourself, etc.)

4. How to be a leader/ lead by example and not be easily swayed- If you have never heard of the saying, " *If you don't stand for something you'll fall for everything"* you have now. People need to learn how to not follow everything and everyone. Learn to be an independent thinker. You don't want someone guiding you down the wrong path to something that could harm you. Do your own

research before you just believe whatever you're told and then later find out it's not actually factual.

5. How to balance a checkbook, budget, manage debt, bargain, use coupons, invest if you choose to and how and when to make a major purchase, file taxes.

6. Survival Skills (Advocate for yourself, first aid, self defense, take public transportation, change a flat tire, check oil, pump gas, how to handle emergency situations,etc. By the way, never let your gas tank go below a certain level-usually a ¼ tank. You don't want to be stranded on the side of the road because you ran out of gas. Get in the habit of checking your tank when you get in your vehicle. Also get your oil changed in your car every 3000-5000 miles)

7. How to prioritize (Make a list if you need to learn the importance. This and time management is going to be important in life, work, health and finding balance between them)

8. Know how to use electronics, technology, etc. (Your alarm clock for example, internet safety,etc.)

9. Contribute (Be a team player- help out when necessary without being asked. If you see something that needs to be done, do it . Examples are things like dishes, laundry,etc. Who's going to do your laundry when you're in college?)

10. Housekeeping Skills (Laundry, cleaning the bathroom, washing dishes, cleaning up after yourself, make your bed, clean their room, sewing, unclog a toilet or sink)

11. Order food/how to calculate a tip/ how to calculate a sales price

12. Plan

13. How to vote.

14. How to effectively communicate (written and verbal communication, public speaking, buy stamps, mail letters and properly address them, simple etiquette, being thoughtful and grateful-writing thank you notes, or talking to someone)

15. How to apply for a job, write a resume and cover letter.

16. How to read a map and have back up physical copy of directions. (I used my phone for directions traveling across the country and when I went through the mountains, I lost the signal. Thank goodness I had a physical copy of directions in the car and a map. Being in the middle of nowhere without cell phone service is no fun at all)

17. How to research things online and at a library (This is a good time to visit the library and obtain a library card. The librarians and very knowledgable and helpful. When students go to college, professors will expect them to already know how to do this. Make a few visits to the library and look things up. It sounds silly, but when you get your first term paper, you will be grateful you did) Note: A lot of academic journals are online, but there are times when nothing but a physical book will do. Embrace it either way.

18. Critical Thinking/ Problem Solving Skills

19. How to process compliments/ criticism.

20. Intrapersonal vs Interpersonal Skills

(Niz, 2016) (Soukup)

CHAPTER 2

Financial Literacy

How can you be expected to be prepared and ready for the next step in adulthood if you can't manage your money? If you haven't been taught? How will you be able to apply for a job, buy food, or use the money you earned to live if you are not at least somewhat aware of how to handle your personal finances? If you don't learn to manage, you will be asking your parents for money all the time. You will at some point have to stand on your two feet. If they don't have it, you'll learn the necessity a lot sooner. Learn to manage now, so later on it will be easier to manage your money as an adult. Adults who don't manage their money end up in debt-debt that can climb to what seems like insurmountable heights. Someone who truly understands does not want to end up in the rat race among many others living outside of their means hoping and praying to get out of debt, or to buy their dream home, but never actually obtaining that dream. Trying to keep up with the latest fashions and the latest and greatest technology on a shoestring budget is tough. It would seem to be more stressful to actually think you need to continually acquire these items than to just budget accordingly and plan out purchases you can't afford at the time. Seriously consider buying when you need them rather than when you just want them. There's nothing wrong with buying things you want on occasion, you just don't need to buy them every time something new comes out just because everyone else has it.

"More than one in six students in the United States failed to reach the baseline level of proficiency in financial literacy." Close to 30,000 teens from 18 countries participated in this initial assessment in financial literacy. American students fell somewhere in the middle in terms of results. This tells us that somewhere along the way, the system is failing students when it comes to financial preparedness (Council For Economic Education, 2016).

The question you're probably wondering is, "What can I do?" The answer for this is quite simple. Don't just sit back and wait because you don't know. Seek answers. If you have parents that are financially responsible and knowledgeable, ask them to teach you their ways. Even if they've tried to teach you and you said you already knew or didn't have time to learn, seek the help because now you know it's important. Most parents are happy to show you what they know about finances. I know it sounds crazy, but that's why talking is so important. If you don't feel like they get you or there seems to be nothing to talk about, ask them questions. It might just open the door of communication. What if you find that you have something in common after all? If your parents don't know about finances, look it up- just like your teacher would tell you in school. What if just maybe you both end up learning how to manage money? There's a plethora of information available to you now, so no more excuses. Start off with simple questions in your search like, how to manage money, budgeting, money management, living within your means. There are so many videos online about budgeting, getting out of debt, etc.

There are many ways to learn about money without actually breaking the bank. Years ago, my children participated in a program through their school that started the groundwork for financial literacy for them. This was a field trip where each class was part of an entire town. They elected a mayor and each child had to apply for a job. They had mock interviews where they were required to dress up and go through the interview process. Students learned about their job, then worked the day in their respective roles. They had mock check books, post offices, ecommerce, etc. It was a quintessential town for these students. They were responsible for running the entire town. They paid for items by writing checks through their fictitious checking accounts and even had to balance their checkbook each time they spent money. What a great way to help students have a bit of insight into the world of business.

That particular program was more than likely specific to certain regions and may not be available everywhere. While this was a great start to what they needed to know, there was more education needed to guide them. Do your research. Find what's available near you or at your fingertips. I can't stress the importance of searching online safely for information like finances and how to manage them.

Here's a list of important things to know along with a few tools and ideas to help you with becoming financially literate. If you have detailed questions, seek the help of a professional financial advisor. This is a tool to help you manage your budget and get you started in the right direction.

1. Create a budget and learn how to manage it. - This includes writing and balancing a checkbook. Many students are happy to spend their parent's or

guardian's money and even their own without regards to a budget. The reality is that the money has to come from somewhere. Most people do not have an endless supply of money. They work hard to earn that money. It's why some students may hear their parents tell them that money doesn't grow on trees. That's because it doesn't. They go to a job every day to bring home money to take care of you. Some of you may even help contribute if you have a job of your own. That paycheck that comes once a week, every two weeks or monthly is how you are provided for. It pays the bills, puts food on the table, pays the electricity, etc. That's not always the case. Some students are very independant and seldom ask for money. The illustrations on page 34 inlude a sample blank check and an endorsed and completed check to show you what goes on each area.

- At some point you will need to open a checking or savings account. If you have earned scholarships that will be awarded to you, then it's a good idea to research a financial institutions to see where you will need to house your money. Some people will choose banks and some may choose a credit union. The choice is yours. You will more than likely not receive this money until after it has been disbursed from the school. Each scholarship is different. Either way, if you are working to save up, you need a place to house your savings. Did you know that there are some scholarships that you can earn as young as 14? Each scholarship has its own guidelines. Donors choose what criteria scholarship applicants must meet in order to be eligible. It's never too early to prepare.

- Important note- **Never** sign your name to a blank check. If you lose the check, anyone can now pick that check up, write it for whatever amount they want and fill in their name. Protect yourself by not doing this. Do not sign the back of a paycheck or any check given to you until you in front of the bank teller ready to deposit. This is for your safety as well. If you drop or lose it and it's signed, someone can easily sign it over to himself or herself and cash it and you are now out of that amount of money. The following illustrations are sample same checks. One is blank. The other has instructions on how to complete a check.

```
Name                                                          976
Address
City, State, Zip Code
                                           DATE: _____
PAY
TO THE
ORDER OF _____ |$ [          ]
_____Dollars
          FINANCIAL INSTITUITION
              CITY, STATE and ZIP

FOR _____      _____
     00976      000000000:      12345678
```

```
                              Name                                  976
                              Address
                              City, State, Zip Code
                                                   DATE: March 1st
                              PAY
This is who the check         TO THE                                         Always write the date
is made payable to.           ORDER OF The person or business you are paying  |$  $17.50
                              Seventeen dollars and 50 cents---------------DOLLARS
                                    FINANCIAL INSTITUITION                   This is where you
Write the dollar amount             CITY, STATE and ZIP                      will write the dollar amount
out here, then add a line
all the way to the end.       FOR _____    Your signature Here
                                   00976    000000000:    12345678
```

This is where you would sign your name

- Another very important note: Do **not** ever write a check for an amount that you know you don't have the money in the bank to cover. If you do this, you are writing a check for what is called insufficient funds. Some people refer to it as bouncing a check or overdrafting. It means you don't have the money in the bank to buy something you bought. This includes buying things over the internet or setting up payments for amounts that you don't have money to cover. Some merchants do not take their money right away from your account. This can throw you off if you are not keeping track. Not knowing this can be a huge hassle. There are fees that will be associated with this and depending on the amount could lead to legal trouble. Insufficient funds will come with fees from the bank or credit union that you will be expected to pay. It will not be for just one check, it will be for each check or transaction you write that takes you below a zero balance. What you have to spend is what you to have to spend. To avoid the headache and embarrassment, do not overspend and do not write checks for money you do not have. The money will not magically appear in your account. Balance your checkbook by writing the amount you spent down in the register and subtracting it from your balance right away. In addition, set a specific amount that you will not let your checkbook balance fall below without good reason. Stick to the amount and don't spend frivolously. I would not expect a college student's balance to be super high. You're learning how to manage your money. Base your amount on what you have and what you need. See the sample below for balancing your account.

Here is a sample checkbook register- one that's blank, one that's been used. Notice I used the check number #976 from the above check and the information to start. Also take a look at the first line on the second checkbook register. It is blank except for the amount. This is done when you are starting a new book or let's say you recently open an account. You would write something similar to opening deposit if it's a new account or carryover balance if it's an existing account in which you used your last register and needed to start a new one- whatever works best for you.

While most of us will not use an actual check unless necessary, you will know how and you will also know how to balance your checkbook. As you read on, you will notice a sample budget as well. You can choose to use that as a way to balance in addition to this or choose one or the other. It all depends on your preference.

Item or Check Number	Date	Transaction Description	Payment / Debit -	Deposit/ Credit +	Balance	

Item or Check Number	Date	Transaction Description	Payment / Debit -	Deposit/ Credit +	Balance	
					$343	15
976	1-Mar	The person or business	$17.50		$325	65
977	2-Mar	Name of Retail Store	$10		$315	65

- Here are some things that I have done to help my kids learn about money: During back to school shopping, I establish a monetary number and that is how much they have to spend on their clothing for the first part of the year. I stopped buying a whole school year at a time when they started growing over the breaks. They have to tally up each item and weigh the cost between how much they have and their desire to have that item. After each store, they take the receipts and keep a running tally of what has been spent so far, so they know what they have left to spend. Unless you have an endless amount of cash flow in college, you can start something similar to this now and continue using this into college. The way it would work for you in high school is to create a budget using the money you receive whether it be from a job or allowance. Write it down, don't rely on memory. Track what comes in and what you spend by writing it down. Hopefully most of you don't have bills right now. If you do, that amount should be deducted from your incoming balance. What you have left is yours to decide what to do. Do you have a savings account to start saving for college?

- Ideas for budgeting: Establish a set amount on what you want to save each month after you've purchased things and/or paid bills. Make it realistic. Example: If you have $150 a month allowance that is what you start with. Establish the amount you will spend on food. Let's say $55 as an estimate of what you might spend monthly on food. You have a meal plan, so this is your extra items that you might keep in your dorm room. This leaves you with $95. If you don't have health and beauty items already (like shampoo,soap,etc), you need to budget in those. Deduct another $30. Now you have $65 left. If your needs are taken care of, this is your discretionary income. Don't spend it all if you don't have to. Bank most of it if you can. Now there will be campus events that will cost money and you might want to attend a few. That's okay, just don't spend your last dime on an event. Keep money aside for emergencies. In this scenario, try to take $50 a month and bank it for emergencies and just general saving. If you saved $50 every month as an example, you could have around $450 by the end of the school year. That is responsible budgeting. It's not totally denying yourself, it's just being wise about what and where you spend money. I have included two samples of budget sheets. I have used both. One is the written form and the other is electronic. I've tried to customize it according to what your budget might resemble. The first example uses $200 as a monthly income.

	Jan-15	Feb-15	Mar-15	Apr-15	May-15	Jun-15	Jul-15	Aug-15	Sep-15	Oct-15	Nov-15	Dec-15	Totals
Paycheck	$200.00	$200.00	$200.00	$200.00	$200.00	$200.00	$200.00	$200.00	$200.00	$200.00	$200.00	$200.00	$2,400.00
SAVINGS	$10.00	$10.00	$10.00	$10.00	$10.00	$10.00	$10.00	$10.00	$10.00	$10.00	$10.00	$10.00	$120.00
Groceries	$80.00	$80.00	$80.00	$80.00	$80.00	$80.00	$80.00	$80.00	$80.00	$80.00	$80.00	$80.00	$960.00
Toiletries	$20.00	$20.00	$20.00	$20.00	$20.00	$20.00	$20.00	$20.00	$20.00	$20.00	$20.00	$20.00	$240.00
Cell Phone	$20.00	$20.00	$20.00	$20.00	$20.00	$20.00	$20.00	$20.00	$20.00	$20.00	$20.00	$20.00	$240.00
Gas/ Transportation	$40.00	$40.00	$40.00	$40.00	$40.00	$40.00	$40.00	$40.00	$40.00	$40.00	$40.00	$40.00	$480.00
Misc.	$10.00	$10.00	$10.00	$10.00	$10.00	$10.00	$10.00	$10.00	$10.00	$10.00	$10.00	$10.00	$120.00
Entertainment	$20.00	$20.00	$20.00	$20.00	$20.00	$20.00	$20.00	$20.00	$20.00	$20.00	$20.00	$20.00	$240.00
													$0.00
													$0.00
													$0.00
Discretionary	$10.00	$10.00	$10.00	$10.00	$10.00	$10.00	$10.00	$10.00	$10.00	$10.00	$10.00	$10.00	$120.00
Total each month	$190.00	$190.00	$190.00	$190.00	$190.00	$190.00	$190.00	$190.00	$190.00	$190.00	$190.00	$190.00	$2,280.00

Bills

Bill	Balance	Payment Amount Due	Due Date	Date Paid	Amount Paid

2. Understand the difference between credit cards and debit cards.

- **Credit cards** are borrowed money. You are given a dollar limit (often times referred to as your credit limit) usually based on your ability and trustworthiness to pay it back. You charge a certain amount on your credit card and that is the balance you owe with interest. The credit card company will request a minimum balance due each month. You should try to pay off the balance in full each month because the remaining balance will still be there with interest added to it. If you go over the limit, there are over the limit fees that you have to pay back. The best bet is to only buy what you can afford to pay back because if you don't, the balance will keep growing and before you know, you will owe more than you can afford to pay.

- **Debit Cards** are attached to your checking account. It's like the electronic way of using a checkbook. Always know your balance, not what

you see in the bank, but your true balance.
Sometimes it takes companies a few days to take
their money from your account. Don't base what
you spend on what the bank shows as your balance.
Keep track of what you deposit into your account
and what you spend. If you spend more than what
you have in the bank, you will have an overdraft fee.
All these things can be avoided if you spend only
what you know you have available.

3. Know how to create a grocery shopping list and how to
shop while staying within budget.

- If you have a meal plan, you will not have a large
  list. If you are in the dorm, what size is your fridge?
  Are you sharing with your roommate? How much
  do you actually have to spend on food? These are all
  questions you have to consider when making a list.
  Let's use the example that you have $50 for
  groceries. Make your list based on what you need
  and want. Needs go before wants. Wants will be

after you have the needs. Create a list based on what you have available currently and go from there.

Here's an example.

Grocery List		
Fruits	Veggies	
Strawberries	Carrots	
Apples	Broccoli	
Oranges	Green Beans	
Breakfast:		
Eggs		
Cereal		
Yogurt		
Lunch & Dinner:		
Rice		
Fish		
Snacks:	Drinks:	Extra:
Salsa, Chips	Tea	

- How to weigh want vs necessity.
- Want is just what it says, you want it. You see the new pair of shoes that just came out and everyone has them but you. You want them because everyone has them and you think they are kind of cool. You have six pairs of shoes in good condition. These would go great with your new outfit you bought at

the mall last week. It's name brand and this would totally make your day. The reality is this is a want, not a need. Now if you have the money, no bills, maybe occasionally you do buy nice things for yourself. That's okay. You just don't have to have the latest of everything because that will leave you broke. Ask yourself how much you have in the bank or saved at home, what do you actually need right now and if you buy it, will you be broke until you get allowance or a paycheck again? Would you rather have money in the bank or would you rather have something you don't really need?

- Necessity (need) is again pretty straight forward. These are things you need like food. Clothing could fall into that category, but the difference is in your why. Why did you buy that new pair of shoes that everyone is talking about? You didn't really need them because you have several pairs. You wanted them. Justifying a want as a need still makes it a want. Try to prioritize your needs over your wants.

- Making wise purchases is key to staying on track with your budget. Knowing when to spend and when not to spend is what will help. This is where want and need might conflict. The fact of the matter is, you will buy some wants and that's okay at times. Learn when it's okay and when you should wait to make a purchase- especially one that will set you back quite a bit. Know your why for spending and know your why for saving. Your why for saving is so that you have money for things you need or if an emergency comes up and to just not be broke. What is your why for spending? Ask yourself when analyzing whether or not you should buy something. Spending small amounts can add up just like large purchases if you are not mindful.

- Planning for financial goals and saving go hand in hand. Think of a financial goal for yourself. I'll use the example of working over the summer and saving for the school year. I love that my husband, boyfriend at the time did this. I wish I had thought to do it myself. He worked hard over the summer to save up for college. He worked a 40 hour a week job and banked most of his money. He was able to make enough over the summer to where he did not have to work during the school year. He was very diligent about depositing his check and spending very little because his goal was to focus on his studies during the school year. He lived at home, so it was already tough enough getting back and forth to school. To add a job on top of that with no vehicle of his own, would have made the situation even tougher. He did this every summer that he could while in college. Some students will work on campus and that's totally fine. Some students will work off campus while attending college, if that works for you, great. The idea is to strategize on a plan to work towards a financial goal. My husband's plan was to not have to work during the school year because he did not have a vehicle of his own at the time. He worked and saved to make that a reality.

- Learn about insurance, investing, retirement accounts, etc.

- Health insurance and life insurance are two important things that you need to make sure you have. Typically your parents will have this (hopefully and if not, get it through your school). The unexpected happens and you need to prepare just in case. Have a conversation about both. Once you are an adult you want to have both. They serve two different purposes. Without health insurance, you will be paying the price set by the health care provider whereas if you have a health insurance, if they are participating with your plan, they have agreed to charge a certain price. It is often times called an allowable amount. You hope you don't have to visit the doctor, but the reality is that sometimes we need to go- even if it's for a check-up.

Save yourself the hassle and try to get coverage if you don't have it.

- Life insurance is something you have for security. If something happens to you or a loved one, life insurance is for peace of mind. It is designed to help with burial expenses. Later on in life, if you are married and your spouse works, if one of you perishes, you would be losing that income. Talk to a professional about what makes sense for you and your family in terms of coverage. These are things to think about when looking at life insurance. Losing someone is never easy. Having to cover burial expenses without coverage is going to add to your stress and grief. That is where the peace of mind comes in.

- I have already started the conversations about retirement accounts and investing with my children. They know that the moment they are eligible through their work for a 401K or some type of retirement account like a 403B , they are to sign up and start as soon as they become eligible. This is important because they will want to have the option to retire at some point. If they choose to continue working past retirement years, that's fine, but having the option is what gives them power.

- We've watch videos to learn and read about investing. Research is always key. Investing is a tricky thing and is never a guarantee. That's why it is so important to research and learn before you do anything. Talk to a financial advisor professional about investing to learn more.

CHAPTER 3

Debt

DEBT- DON'T ENTER BY TEMPTATION

There is no fancy necessity behind the definition of debt. It is when you owe money.

Your typical college students enters college debt free. They usually graduate with debt in the form of student loans. The number starts off seemingly small, but by the time they graduate it can be astronomical- especially if you add in advanced degrees. I'm not completely against student loans. In many cases, they are necessary. How would we have doctors, attorneys, dentists and professors to name a few without the use of student loans if scholarships don't cover it all? We wouldn't because not everyone has the money readily available to outright pay for college. Medical school is a long process that is not cheap. We need good doctors. The same goes for attorneys and educators and many other fields. We need them, so some students will acquire debt while in college, graduate, law or medical school.

When I say don't enter into debt by temptation, I am referring to a few different things. One of those is credit cards. I could not count the number of students who were tempted by the cool t-shirt, water bottle or other items free when they sign up for a credit card. Those tables are designed to grab your attention and give you a magic card with money. Remember you have to pay it back. It seems easy and full of potential benefits until the balance gets too high to afford because you didn't pay off last month's bill like you planned or the month before. Don't be fooled. If you are going to use credit cards, be wise. Most people will have a credit card. They are not terrible if used wisely. It's again one of those things where you have to decide what works for you.

If you're going to have a card, don't overspend. Do not be tempted to buy the new wardrobe you want because you think the clothes you have aren't good enough. Do not be tempted by the free items you get just for applying. Use the card wisely if you decide to have one. Don't be tempted to easily give out your personal information either. Remember that the information you give to receive the card will be associated with you on your credit report. If you do not pay on time, it will be reported to the 3 repositories. The repositories are the reporting agencies for credit. They report what type of borrower you are. Your credit limit along with how much you owe will also be on your credit report. It's important to try to keep your balance under 35% if you keep a recurring balance (A balance that stays on the card month to month). The repositories are the bureaus who essential store your credit information. You will have a FICO score (FAIR ISAAC Company) based on your performance with credit. This will tell potential creditors if you are creditworthy and how big of a risk you are. Your credit score will be essential when trying to buy a car, a home or even to rent a place. Keep your score in good standing. If you damage it, it can be repaired through diligence on your part to get it where it needs to be. Pay your bills on time and do not live outside of your means. Do your best to live under your means. It means not spending every bit and more of what money you have coming in on things you don't need. Keep your debt to a minimum. Borrow when you need to, not necessarily when you want to.

Here are two examples of ways to save and budget. One focuses on budgeting your money and the other focuses on keeping track of your bills. Some people prefer simplicity while others prefer a little more elaborate. Here is the more elaborate. It shows a hypothetical amount a student might receive, how much is saved and what expenses students might incur.

	B Jan-15	C Feb-15	D Mar-15	E Apr-15	F May-15	G Jun-15	H Jul-15	I Aug-15	J Sep-15	K Oct-15	L Nov-15	M Dec-15	N Totals
Paycheck	$200.00	$200.00	$200.00	$200.00	$200.00	$200.00	$200.00	$200.00	$200.00	$200.00	$200.00	$200.00	$2,400.00
SAVINGS	$10.00	$10.00	$10.00	$10.00	$10.00	$10.00	$10.00	$10.00	$10.00	$10.00	$10.00	$10.00	$120.00
Groceries	$80.00	$80.00	$80.00	$80.00	$80.00	$80.00	$80.00	$80.00	$80.00	$80.00	$80.00	$80.00	$960.00
Toiletries	$20.00	$20.00	$20.00	$20.00	$20.00	$20.00	$20.00	$20.00	$20.00	$20.00	$20.00	$20.00	$240.00
Cell Phone	$20.00	$20.00	$20.00	$20.00	$20.00	$20.00	$20.00	$20.00	$20.00	$20.00	$20.00	$20.00	$240.00
Gas/ Transportation	$40.00	$40.00	$40.00	$40.00	$40.00	$40.00	$40.00	$40.00	$40.00	$40.00	$40.00	$40.00	$480.00
Misc.	$10.00	$10.00	$10.00	$10.00	$10.00	$10.00	$10.00	$10.00	$10.00	$10.00	$10.00	$10.00	$120.00
Entertainment	$20.00	$20.00	$20.00	$20.00	$20.00	$20.00	$20.00	$20.00	$20.00	$20.00	$20.00	$20.00	$240.00
													$0.00
													$0.00
													$0.00
Discretionary	$10.00	$10.00	$10.00	$10.00	$10.00	$10.00	$10.00	$10.00	$10.00	$10.00	$10.00	$10.00	$120.00
Total each month	$190.00	$190.00	$190.00	$190.00	$190.00	$190.00	$190.00	$190.00	$190.00	$190.00	$190.00	$190.00	$2,280.00

This spreadsheet is for someone who might have bills that need to be paid. Here's a guide to helping organize and pay debt. I successfully used this system below for a number of years.

Bills					
Bill	Balance	Payment Amount Due	Due Date	Date Paid	Amount Paid

CHAPTER 4

College Testing

Some high school counselors will advise you against taking the ACT and/or SAT before your junior year. Some will tell you that it's fine to take it whenever you like. Their concern when they advise against taking it early is that you will not have been introduced to many of the math concepts on the test. Their concern is valid. By tenth grade, you will not have been introduced to many of the concepts and therefore may score lower than expected. You also have to pay for the test as many times as you take it, though some school districts are covering the charge for juniors. Those are important things to take into consideration.

While it is true that students don't have all the math before 11th grade, I still recommend thinking through whether it is beneficial for you to wait to take the exam for the first time. My suggestion is simple. Take the test anyway. There are many ways to prepare for this test. Check to see if your school or area offers and ACT/SAT boot camps or workshop to prepare you. You can study online and take a series of practice exams in addition to finding a workshop. Some homework help facilities might offer ACT prep as well as schools. The more practice you get on this, the better your chances for increasing your score. Make sure that you research to find reputable places in your area before spending money. You want to make sure it is a good investment. It's always good to invest in yourself, it's just that you want to make sure the company is who they say they are.

Base your decision on how to prepare based on your ability to take and retake the test because you do have to pay each time you take the exam in most cases- except in those districts where they cover the cost for juniors. Take your results, then find the best way to improve unless of course your score is perfect. The reason for considering taking the test early is to see where you need the most help and then add extra focus on those areas to increase your score. That may mean tutoring or going online to free tutorial sites. It could be that you can just reach out to your teacher and ask for help. Each scenario is going to be different. Adjust accordingly.

Again, students will more than likely not have been introduced to all the concepts, especially in math, but to be completely honest, you still may not be introduced to all the concepts on the test regardless. It's time to start researching your options. Taking the test early can help students with the stress of having to make the test count on their first try. If you or your student waits to take the test, the pressure may be greater on them to perform versus planning and retaking as necessary.

There are programs out there designed to give students sample exams that closely resemble the actual test, review the results with them and then tutor in the areas that need tutoring. These programs typically cost money, but research your area to see what is available. You may find similar programs in your area for free or a small fee. There's also the world wide web. In addition, there are places online where you can learn more academically. Never rely solely on public education to teach you. Supplement when and how you can and use your resources.

Sometimes university and college towns have tutoring available for lower rates. These tends to be more of a single subject tutoring program, but you have to find what works for you and your family. If you live near a college or university, visit their website and search for tutoring, teaching, lessons, or anything closely related to this. Often times, there will be a tiered pricing structure: undergraduate students will give lessons, graduate students and professors or masters of the field. These lessons range from musical to academic quite frequently. In some cases, there are group lessons which lower the price. Finances always need to be taken into consideration.

Make your determination based on what you and your family can afford and check for scholarship options and waivers with these programs.

Once you've decided whether or not you can take the test early, plan accordingly. Depending on where you want to go to school will determine which or if both tests are required (referring to ACT or SAT). There are far too many schools to attempt to tell you which one requires what. The best thing to do is to go to your choice schools and search for their requirements.

It may sound strange to start this process early, but you will find that you are able to plan easier when you know in advance. For example, if you take the ACT in the fall and the SAT in the spring of your sophomore year and then switch the order by taking the SAT in the fall and the ACT in the spring of the following year, you now have taken them both twice. Hopefully your score will have increased and you won't have to take them again. If you need to take them again, you've given yourself options as to when to take them and you've more than likely taken a little bit of stress off yourself by planning in advance.

Some college applications are due in the middle of the fall season while others give you till the first of the year. If you want to or need to take the test again, you have the summer of junior year or possibly an early fall of your senior year to take the test. It is critical to check the application deadlines at each school you plan to apply to to determine when applications are due. Often times you want your test results back before you apply. When looking for college application deadlines, check for requirements for submission as well.

CHAPTER 5

College Visits

Typically, most students begin visiting their prospective college campuses during their junior year. The time to start looking at colleges is somewhere around 10th grade, so that you can be ready to visit junior year. Note that you can visit your sophomore year as well. Pick somewhere around 3-5 colleges at least to visit. If the decision is tough and you want to visit more, by all means visit more. It does mean you will have to plan out the visits more strategically to fit them all in.

You might want to consider making a second visit if the school is reasonably local. By seeing it a second time, you can begin to eliminate schools you don't want to attend or solidify the decision to attend a certain school. If your school choice is contingent upon scholarship options, this is particularly important. Find out all you can about the schools you've opted to consider attending.

With regards to scholarships, get the details of your award offers as well. Sometimes what you may think is a full ride scholarship (all inclusive paid education) is a mixture of things that do not always include free. Grants are free money. You do not have to pay grants back. You do need to look at the stipulations to make certain you meet the criteria. Make certain you research your responsibilities you need to maintain in order to make certain grants remain free money and not an obligation you have to pay back later because you did not follow the guidelines. Student loans are not free, they are required to be paid back.

One might wonder how I know so much about student loans, grants and scholarships. I worked for years in education - a large portion of that time at the collegiate level. Prior to that, I experienced the downfalls first hand and have since learned from them.

The first college I attended was supposed to be a full athletic scholarship, or at least I was under the impression that it was. I had a few choices in schools and I made the decision I thought would best benefit me. I did not find out when I signed my letter of intent. I found out over the summer when my financial aid officer reached out to me that I was not getting what I thought was a "full ride".

My work study job was cleaning my uniform and my teammates' uniforms. Now, I didn't have a problem with humility where it was an issue to wash uniforms and practice jerseys of my own and my teammates, the issue was that I was not informed and I was the only one on the team who had work study so far as I knew. Playing a college sport, going to college and working a job is no easy feat. I don't mention this because I want sympathy. I'm so far over this I tell you. It's that I want to stress to you the importance of reading the fine line details so that you can make a sound decision and one that is best for you. Don't be afraid to ask questions if you don't understand. Even if you do understand, ask clarifying questions to make sure that what you understand is what it actually is.

Once you've done the necessary research, make a list of the pros and cons of each on a sheet of paper. This is where you list your college choices and weigh out the benefits and disadvantages of each. This should include academic, campus, amenities, financial and or other things that are important to you. Remember to research realistic things that are actually important to you. I can't stress that enough. Lay the sheets of paper out, each side by side and compare and contrast. If you are ready to eliminate, you can begin now. If you're not ready, get more details until you can rank your choices. It may mean that you apply to the 3-5 schools you choose, especially if you are uncertain and the deadlines are approaching. That's alright as well. Each scenario will vary. Know your why in choosing a school.

The main thing is to not put all your eggs in one basket. Some schools have the option for students to apply for free or for a discounted amount depending on income. Check with your guidance counselor to see if they have details. Keep in mind that in some situations, you may need to research this information yourself. You all can't have the best counselor like my oldest had. She was instrumental in helping us find the best opportunity for college.

This is the best time to start looking at the types of accreditations schools hold and why that is important. There are two types of accreditations when it comes to colleges and universities: Regional (the most widely recognized) and National. National can be broken down into two categories- faith based (a school with a religious affiliation) and career related. This is important when considering some professional licensing like the field of education. One of the requirements when I obtained my teaching license was that the degree that qualified me to become a teacher, had to be earned at a regionally accredited college or university. There are some professions where this is really important and you need to be made aware of that as you choose a college.

The Council for Higher Education Accreditation (CHEA) is the external organization that reviews the quality of a colleges or universities to ensure it meets certain guidelines. In the United States, accreditation evaluations are performed by a private, non profit organization. Colleges and universities want to prove that the education they provide meets the quality and reputable standards so that students will want to attend their school. In addition, they want this accreditation so that they are eligible for federal funding. (Council for Higher Education Accreditation, 2017)

One type of accreditation is not better than the other typically, you just need to be made of aware of what your career path suggest and requires. Let's compare accreditations so that you have a better understanding of the differences:

Regional Accreditation

- Is the most widely recognized type of accreditation.

- Credits are accepted more when or if you transfer schools.

- Tuition reimbursements from your employer will sometimes require this type of accreditation.

- Some professional licensures like teaching, health care fields and counseling require this. Depending on the profession, there may be other accreditations and curriculum needed, so ask your college counselors.

- Most state colleges and universities fall into this accreditation.

National Accreditation

- Credits are not accepted as easily when or if you transfer schools.

- May cost less because the classes tend to be career oriented- like earning a vocational education. It's not always the case. It really depends on the school.

- Some faith based schools fall into this accreditation.

For more information on how this works, you can always research the Council for Higher Education Accreditation online. (Council for Higher Education Accreditation, 2017)

Community College

Another option that some students consider is going to a community college before attending a four year institution. They do this because it's cheaper. Community colleges typically fall into the regional accreditation classification, so classes transfer a lot easier. They usually are non residential colleges where you stay at home versus living on campus. Sometimes referred to as junior colleges, a lot of students elect to go this route to take as many general education courses as possible before transferring to a four year college to take their major courses. If this is something you choose to do, by all means don't think of it as not attending college or be any less enthusiastic about your choice. You need to find the most affordable way to attend college. If you have scholarships that you've earned or won, be sure to check qualifications-though I've found that a lot of students are able to attend a two-year college or a four-year college and use the scholarship money at either. Just read the guidelines and do what is required.

CHAPTER 6

Financial Aid & Selective Services- males

If you are a male attending college, you are required to register for selective services once you reach 18 years of age. You will not be able to receive federal aid without registering. Both Pell grants and student loans require you register with selective service in order to receive benefits. Selective service is an agency of the government set in place in the event that the United States has to call upon its citizens and eligible non citizens for military enlistment or draft. Males between the age of 18 and 25 are required to register. If you are a male, whether your plan is to immediately attend college right out of high school or work for a while, you are required to register.

In my experience as a counselor at a university years ago, I came across many cases of men who did not register right away. Many of them were not made aware that this was a requirement because they did not attend college right out of high school. By not registering, you lessen your chances of receiving aid because it is a requirement. The process to try to attend college after not registering early on and being over the age of 25 is incredibly difficult. This is a decision young adult males must make for themselves, I only advise the requirements so that you can make an informed decision.

Financial aid has grade point average (gpa) and time frame requirements. You must maintain a minimum gpa in order to continue to be eligible for financial aid. You must also be progressing through your academic program. If your grades fall below a certain level, you could potentially be placed on academic probation. After that, if you are not able to bring your grades up, you could lose eligibility to receive aid and have to leave school. The same is true with academic progression. Colleges and universities may have a different name for it at each school, but it essentially is the same rule- you must be progressing academically in order to keep aid. Keep in mind that you can take elective courses. This is sometimes how college students come to find their passion when they are undeclared (they have not chosen a degree). They take a class that sparks their interest and the rest is history. When we talk about academic progression, I'm moreless for example referring to someone who has exceeded in excess the amount of credits required for their degree, but they have not taken the classes needed for their own degree program. Thus not successfully progressing towards their academic degree. Because this can be an issue, I provide another example of how this can happen later in the chapter and what can be a potential outcome.

Some students are given the opportunity to appeal. In some cases, depending on the circumstance, students are given a chance to redeem themselves but in other situations they are not. The best thing to do is to do your best to keep your grades up while in college by doing your best. It sounds so trivial I know, but it's really quite that simple. I'm not implying college is easy because it's not. I'm simply saying that you have to do the work. If you've ever heard of someone flunking out of college, this is typically what they are referring to. Going to college is not exactly like high school. If you don't do well, you may not continue to attend college and it may not be of your own choice.

A student who has been under the wing of a parent for their formative years must now learn to advocate for themselves. That means if you are having trouble in class, it is the student's responsibility, not your parents to go talk to the professors. Ask for help. The professor's job is to teach. You don't need to remind them of their job. They know why they are there. You just need to ask them or the TA (Teacher Assistant) for help. At the collegiate level, they are fully aware of their role. Besides, it will not go over well if you take that approach. If the professor is not available (perhaps it's a large school), then see if they have an assistant in the department who can help. Your first step begins with reaching out to the professor. They cannot read your mind to know what you are thinking, what you are having trouble with or the reason why an assignment was late. You have to communicate and follow up and you need to do it at the first sign of trouble. It's your grade, not theirs. If you asked a professor for something like a document as an example and they agreed to give or send it, if you have not received it in a reasonable time frame, it's your responsibility to follow up with them. Find a system like journaling or marking your calendar for reminders so that you don't forget. These things could make the difference between passing and failing in some instances. Once you're in college, you are the adult, you now need to do all the things your parents did for you or told you to do- the exception is, you need to do it without being told to do it. This was a digression from financial aid, but totally related because your grades can affect your financial aid.

Another way to lose financial aid eligibility is not to progress timely through a program. If a student is taking class after class, but not progressing towards earning a degree or certificate they may be in jeopardy of losing their financial aid. This can happen with students who change their major often. I know they are just trying to figure it all out, but there comes a time when they need to make a decision. Don't be afraid to change your major if you need to, but just be aware that being a career major changer may raise a red flag to the administrative staff.

Here's a situation that Jess experienced that jeopardized her eligible for financial aid. Jess attended college right after high school. She had little guidance from her parents because they just were not well informed. Jess transferred to her fourth school where she met and fell in love with a guy named Chris. Chris was great. Jess decided that because Chris was so great, she was going to spending every waking moment with him. Instead of going to class, she skipped over and over until she eventually failed the semester.

Still in love, she continued to skip classes, but actually attended on occasion. Her grades, quality of work and attendance were so poor that Jess failed all of her classes again. Now she was faced with two semesters of poor performance. She was placed on academic probation. To top it off, Jess and Chris broke up. He wanted her to be more independant and succeed. He felt as though she didn't want him to reach his goals of being an orthodontist because she just wanted to hang out.

Jess was so distraught, but she knew she didn't want to flunk out of school. She did not perform well at all that next semester and had to appeal losing her aid. She was not given the chance to redeem herself because she'd already had the opportunity when she was placed on academic probation. She had no choice but to leave school for a while and enter the workforce.

After five years working day after day in a job that she just didn't care for, Jess had finally discovered her calling. She went back to college to try it a second time. Because she did not default on her student loans while out of school (she made her student loan payments) , she was eligible to put them in deferment while she went back to college to earn a degree. Jess had well over 100 credits before attending the local community college. She wanted to start there first before she earned her bachelor degree. This time around, Jess made the dean's list 3 consecutive semesters. Her fourth semester she did just as well in school. Her final semester was her fifth semester. She had to extend her time in school because the class she needed to graduate was not available, but that fifth semester was set to be her final term.

She was advised by her academic counselor that she was going to have to appeal her financial aid eligibility. This baffled her because she knew she did well each semester. The counselor explained that even though her grades were exceptional, she had so many credits from her previous college experience (the ones she passed before meeting Chris) that she needed to appeal. This is sometimes referred to as *satisfactory academic progress*. Jess prepared as advised. The time came for Jess to appeal her aid. She sat in a room full of students, some in the same situation, some with academic warnings and probations. The tension was pretty thick in the room. Not many people spoke. They just sat waiting to be called up to discuss the situation quietly with someone.

As they called Jess' name to come up and present the information, she did. She sat down taking a big gulp trying to clear the knot forming in her throat. The representative looked at her transcript and read the long explanation that Jess provided as to why she had so many credits at a community college and no degree. She explained that the upcoming term would be her final term, the reason why she did not succeed the first time, and that her grades were great since returning after essentially growing up. Jess was granted the exception to receive aid for the term and continue her studies. She graduated with honors from the community college and then went on to earn her four year degree.

The point of this story is to point out that there can be extenuating situations that take you off course. Failing grades may not always be why a student loses their aid. Read and stay informed. Ask questions even if you feel as though it's a stupid question. If you need an answer, ask. This is your future, don't be timid about the things that concern your success.

When you are applying for federal financial aid, you will be applying through the FAFSA. That's the free application for federal student aid. Please be cautious when searching for this online. There are websites out there with similar urls designed to obtain your personal information and money. The FAFSA is the FREE APPLICATION FOR FEDERAL STUDENT AID. If you have to pay, you are not on the right website. Check in with your financial aid department to make sure you are applying to the correct site. Each college typically has a tab or section specifically for financial aid. You should be able to find it directly through the school versus just searching for it. Each school will also have a financial aid department that you can call for information as well.

Funds

Be aware of the type of money you receive for financial aid. In other words, know if you are receiving grants, loans or scholarships. Know whether or not you have to pay it back. It is possible to receive a combination of both. Read the fine print and ask questions about the things you don't understand. A student could receive a few types of financial aid or a combination of them. The following are the typical types of financial aid received while in college: grants, scholarships, loans and military aid. See the definitions below and become familiar with them early on. Notice the difference in them and as you prepare for college, determine what type of aid you receive when you complete your fafsa (free application for federal student aid). Read the definitions below of typical terms.

Financial Aid- *Monetary assistance given through loans, grants, scholarships to students to cover educational expenses.*

Grant- *Money that has been given to you. It is traditionally money you do not have to pay back. Usually is considered need based, meaning you have to meet a certain income guideline to qualify. There are state and federal grants. It is disbursed after a certain time.*

Scholarship- *Money earned in the form of a grant or payment usually awarded based on an achievement. This* is a type of financial aid that can be merit, athletic, knowledge, contest or even cultural.

Military Aid- Money the government offers in the form of military aid to those who has served in the armed forces and opted for this benefit for educational expenses. Sometimes it can be passed down to a descent. Benefit details will vary and need to be verified. One would follow through the process if this was applicable to them.

Student Loans- This is loan money that is given to you in the form of a disbursement. You are required to pay this money back.

Subsidized Loans- Loan money disbursed to you. While you are in school, the interest does not accrue, but when you graduate or quit school, interest begins to accrue and you are required to pay this money back after a certain time period.

Unsubsidized Loans- Loan money disbursed to you. Interest starts to accrue on this right away once you borrow it, but you are not required to pay it back until you either graduate or quit school.

Stafford Loans- Need-based government loans that are given to a college or university student after tuition and any fees have been paid. If Stafford loans are used, repayment is not required until after the student graduates or leaves school.

Perkins Loans- A low-interest loan *awarded to both undergraduate and graduate students who have a great deal of financial need. The school is the actual lender of a Perkins loan, so repayments are made directly to the school. Repayments on a Perkins loan begins nine months after they have graduated or leave school.*

PLUS Loans- Low-interest loans *that are paid directly to the parents of the student. The money is borrowed on* behalf of the student, but it still goes to the parents to help pay educational expenses.

Disbursement- When the school pays out or give you money whether it be a loan or a grant. Students receive what is left typically each term after your educational expenses are paid for that term. Disbursements typically happen by the quarter or semester after a certain amount of time.

Refund- The amount remaining after a student's balance has been paid. Some schools split the amount refunded to you up and give it to you over the course of time.

Award Letter- This is a statement that will disclose the type of financial aid you qualify for. It is very common to see some students qualify for a combination of loans, grants and scholarships whereas some may only qualify for loans.

Need Based- *Based on a certain criteria typically decided by your level of financial need.*

Keep in mind that anything that is a loan, needs to be paid back. I know I've said it several times, but that is because it's important. If you drop out and do not finish college, you still will be expected to pay the amount you borrowed back with interest. Take what you need based on your situation and decline the rest. If you take the maximum because it is given to you in loans, you may be excited now, but later on you will be asking yourself why you took out all of that money when you didn't really need it. Take what you need, but don't go overboard. Seniors in high school.. this is the time to calculate your expenses, needs and other resources. What sources of income will you have? For example, allowance. How much is the allowance and how frequently will it be received? What types of expenses will you have each month? Do you have a surplus supply of health and beauty items like shampoo, soap, etc. or do you buy as you go? Do you have transportation to and from the stores to get what you need? This is where my suggestion for planning in advance will be helpful. No one plan works for everyone. Some students move across the country for school and cannot go home every weekend to stock up.

When I went to college, I did not have my own car. I had a ride, but sometimes you just want to have your own things. I learned from that experience that planning ahead is critical. With modern technology, there's also the advantage of buying online and having things shipped. This may be an option for those who do not have a way back and forth to the store, but you have to plan it out.

Look for scholarships to avoid as much as you can in student loans. Look for legitimate scholarships. There are so many available. Students don't apply because they don't think they qualify. I understand the idea that you must qualify for certain scholarships, but every now and then people who qualify don't realize they qualify and they don't apply leaving that scholarship open for submission. Apply! If you don't get it, you are out of a little time spent on maybe an essay and the time it took you to complete the application, but if by chance you are awarded the scholarship you're in luck.

Check local businesses, big name companies, organizations, your school district (check the websites and ask your school counselor). Also look on line. The internet is constantly evolving, so be mindful of where you put your information by making certain it is a legitimate website and company. Don't keep your search just local. Look at well known companies as well. These companies often times will have scholarships. These are tax deductions for them at the end of year, so they tend to be generous. The key to this is to start your search early. Do not wait until the last minute because the deadlines will be come and go.

People in the community sometimes donate money to certain scholarships. It's either in memory of someone or as a way to give back to their community. Some local PTA groups offer scholarships as well. Use the resources around you like your family. Look on their employer's websites or ask. You never know until you ask. If you happen to earn a scholarship that pays for your a large portion of your academic program, you can still apply for outside scholarships.

There are need based scholarships which are exactly what they say, they are based on your financial need. There are merit based which are scholarships where you earn it based usually on academic success. When you are applying for merit based scholarships, do not talk yourself out of applying just because you don't have the highest gpa. There are other criteria used in conjunction with grades to make a final determination.

Your best shot at winning some of these scholarships come when you plan ahead of time and submit quality work. For example, if there is an essay, do your best. Start your search early. Ask someone to proofread the essays for errors. Also read it yourself. I find it easier to print it, read it and make notes because I tend to catch more of my errors versus just looking at it on the screen. For some reason my errors tend to jump right off the page when I print and proofread. I then go in and make the corrections, print again and then ask for someone else to read it.

Here's a little something I learned from one of my fraternity brothers. Search months in advance for scholarships. In fact look the year before just to see what's out there. Just kidding, I knew that already. Seriously though, here's what he said that was pure gold. A highschool student doing this by themselves will get overwhelmed in a matter of minutes. Make a list of what scholarships you want to apply for along with their due dates and requirements. Set calendar reminders for when to apply for certain ones so you meet the deadline. You will increase your chances of earning more money for school by doing this. Create a spreadsheet or use the one on page 90 to track your scholarship due dates and requirements.

**Note: It is so important to not just sign financial documents and accept what is given to you. One thing to consider is to ask the financial aid officer for a little guidance. Though they may not be able to suggest a certain amount, they can advise what current students are doing or what students who wanted to limit the amount of student loan debt they were acquiring. If you decide to take out the full amount the first term because you don't know what to expect, monitor your spending as closely as possible to see what you actually spent. That way the next term if you need to take out loans, you will only take what you need and nothing more. This is not the time to go out and get a new wardrobe. It's enticing, I know. Be frugal when looking at what you need, but be realistic. If you have parents that know about these things, consult them. Another important thing that most students don't know is that even if you accept the entire loan disbursement awarded to you, you can return some of that money. You will want to make sure you have a receipt or proof of returning it so that you are not responsible for money you did not borrow and keep. To build on that, keep your award letters each term until you graduate in a safe place. I would suggest you look at the total when it's time to start paying back student loans to make sure things lined up. Here is a way to track your

scholarships.

Scholarship	Type	Source	Due Date	Requirements	Completed
Sample: Your School District	Merit	School Website	30-Nov	3.5 gpa, 500 word essay	Yes

CHAPTER 7

Packing List

So you're finally ready to start your packing list. There is much debate about when to start this process, but I am of the mindset that preparation is key. Anytime procrastination is the root cause of anything, whether it be time, money, sleep, energy or something else, it typically costs you more than it would if you prepared in advance. My plan was to actively prepare for the upcoming school year in advance, so I was not scrambling last minute to find things. I found several lists in my research and combined them together along with the things I'd already written down. I've left some space at the bottom to fill in additional things you might need. I began the process at the beginning of my student's senior year. I was done about ¾ of the way through the year. I had everything stacked in the stackable bins. Talk about relief when I could actually say I was done prepping and buying. Here's a list to help you start planning.

Room (Dorm rooms are notoriously small, so be mindful as you plan, purchase and pack.)

- ☐ Alarm clock

- ☐ Adhesive hooks and strips

- ☐ Bed side lamp

- ☐ Closet organizer

- ☐ Desk lamp

- ☐ Dry erase board and dry erase markers

- ☐ Fire-proof small safe (to hold jewelry and/ or important papers)

- ☐ Full-length mirror (if there is not one on the door)

- ☐ Hangers

- ☐ Jewelry box or organizer

- ☐ Photos

- ☐ Picture frames or photo clips

- ☐ Rug

- ☐ Shoe rack, shelves or cubby to stack in closet and stack shoes for storage

- ☐ Storage trunk

- ☐ Storage containers
- ☐ Wall art
- ☐ Waste basket or trash can
- ☐
- ☐

Bedding

- ☐ Blankets (quantity of 2- typically space heaters are not permitted, so buy a few warm blankets)
- ☐ Comforter
- ☐ Foam topper
- ☐ Mattress pad
- ☐ Mattress cover- protect against bed bugs
- ☐ Pillowcases
- ☐ Pillows
- ☐ Sleeping bag or air mattress (optional, only after you have necessities are covered- college kids do still have slumber parties)
- ☐ Throw pillows or bed rest pillow (they will not always work at their desk and a cold wall is not comfortable)

- ☐ Twin XL bed sheets (typically dorm beds are XL, but check with the dorm prior to buying- quantity of 2)
- ☐
- ☐

Laundry

- ☐ Bleach
- ☐ Drying rack
- ☐ Fabric sheets
- ☐ Iron or steamer
- ☐ Laundry detergent
- ☐ Lingerie bag
- ☐ Lint brush
- ☐ Quarters (If the laundry machines are coin operated or electronic cards on campus)
- ☐ Sewing kit
- ☐ Stain remover
- ☐ Small ironing board

- ☐ Small stackable laundry baskets or stackable bins for laundry (You'll need 3 to separate clothes by lights, darks and whites after wear. Buy small bins or baskets so students will get in the habit of not letting the baskets overfill. There's not as much room at school at there is at home and they do have to share the space with another individual typically. Educate your child on this and how to be considerate.)
- ☐ Wrinkle release (this spray is amazing for when you do not have time to iron.)
- ☐ Traveling tote on wheels
- ☐
- ☐

Bathroom

- ☐ Air freshener
- ☐ Bath towels (quantity of 5 or less)
- ☐ Bathrobe

- ☐ Bathroom cleaning supplies (all purpose disinfectant cleaner, gloves and sponge just in case)
- ☐ Shower caddy
- ☐ Shower cap
- ☐ Shower shoes
- ☐ Washcloths (quantity of 5 or less)
- ☐
- ☐

Toiletries

- ☐ Body wash or bath soap
- ☐ Chapstick
- ☐ Conditioner
- ☐ Deodorant
- ☐ Eye cream, face cream, gel, etc.
- ☐ Face wash or soap
- ☐ Hair gel and/ or mousse
- ☐ Hairspray
- ☐ Hair care (any additional types of hair care products)

- ❑ Lotion

- ❑ Makeup

- ❑ Makeup remover

- ❑ Moisturizer

- ❑ Mouthwash

- ❑ Nail polish

- ❑ Nail polish remover

- ❑ Shampoo

- ❑ Shaving Cream

- ❑ Sunscreen

- ❑ Toothpaste

- ❑ Wax (if applicable)

- ❑

- ❑

Additional Health and Beauty Supplies

- ❑ Blow dryer

- ❑ Bobby pins

- ❑ Comb

- ❑ Cotton balls

- ❑ Cotton swabs
- ❑ Curling iron, flat iron (any heat related device needed such as hot rollers, etc.)
- ❑ Diffusers
- ❑ Eyeglass (cleaners, cases, contact lens and cleaners, etc.)
- ❑ Feminine hygiene products (pads & tampons)
- ❑ Floss
- ❑ Hairbrush
- ❑ Headbands
- ❑ Mirror
- ❑ Nail clippers set (file,clippers,scrubbers,etc)
- ❑ Ponytail Scrunchies
- ❑ Razor
- ❑ Round brush
- ❑ Sunglasses
- ❑ Sweatbands
- ❑ Tissues
- ❑ Toilet paper
- ❑ Toothbrush

- ☐ Toothbrush holder
- ☐ Tweezers
- ☐
- ☐

Medical

- ☐ Birth control
- ☐ First aid kit (antiseptic wipes, cream or spray, aspirin, ibuprofen, bandaids, hot pack/ cold pack)
- ☐ Humidifier
- ☐ Insect repellent
- ☐ Lozenges (sore throat, cough- use your best judgement)
- ☐ Medicine (use your best judgement- anti diarrhea, etc.)
- ☐ Prescription medicine
- ☐ Prescription refill information
- ☐ Rubbing alcohol
- ☐ Thermometer
- ☐ Thermometer covers

- ☐ Throat spray
- ☐ Upset stomach medication
- ☐ Vaseline
- ☐ Vitamins
- ☐
- ☐

Kitchen Supplies

- ☐ Bottle opener
- ☐ Broom
- ☐ Can opener
- ☐ Chip clips
- ☐ Dish towels
- ☐ Dishes (bowls, plates, cups)
- ☐ Dishwashing soap
- ☐ Disinfecting wipes
- ☐ Duster
- ☐ Dustpan
- ☐ Glass cleaner
- ☐ Hand soap

- [ ] Microwave (if your school allows it)
- [ ] Mini fridge (if your school allows it)
- [ ] Mini vacuum
- [ ] Mugs
- [ ] Oven mitt
- [ ] Paper plates
- [ ] Paper towels
- [ ] Plastic wrap
- [ ] Reusable water bottle
- [ ] Sealable plastic bags
- [ ] Sponges
- [ ] Tin foil
- [ ] Toaster (if your school allows it)
- [ ] Trash bags
- [ ] Travel mug
- [ ] Tupperware
- [ ] Utensils
- [ ] Water filter pitcher
- [ ]
- [ ]

Technical Things

- ☐ Batteries

- ☐ Camera

- ☐ Computer or laptop (bring all things required for setup)

- ☐ Chargers (phone, laptop, camera, etc.)

- ☐ Flash drive

- ☐ Headphones

- ☐ Lap desk

- ☐ Portable phone charger

- ☐ Printer

- ☐ Printer ink

- ☐ Printer paper

- ☐ Recording device for lectures

- ☐ SD card for camera

- ☐ Surge protectors

- ☐ TV (check with the roommate)

- ☐

- ☐

Desk/School Supplies

- ☐ Address book
- ☐ Accordion folder
- ☐ Backpack
- ☐ Binders
- ☐ Calculator
- ☐ Calendar
- ☐ Desk organizer
- ☐ Envelopes
- ☐ Glue
- ☐ Highlighters
- ☐ Hole punch
- ☐ Paper (any and all- notebook, notepads, post its, journals, index cards, etc.)
- ☐ Pencil sharpener
- ☐ Pencils, pens, etc.
- ☐ Planner
- ☐ Post-it notes
- ☐ Postage stamps

- ☐ Printer
- ☐ Stationery items
- ☐ Tape
- ☐ Three-hole punch
- ☐ Wite-Out
- ☐
- ☐

Kitchen Supplies

- ☐ Bottle opener
- ☐ Broom, dustpan, duster
- ☐ Can opener
- ☐ Chip clips
- ☐ Dishes, dish towels, dish soap
- ☐ Disinfecting wipes
- ☐ Hand soap
- ☐ Microwave (if school permits this)
- ☐ Mini fridge (if school permits this)
- ☐ Mug
- ☐ Oven mitt

- ☐ Paper towels

- ☐ Plastic wrap

- ☐ Reusable water bottle

- ☐ Sealable plastic bags

- ☐ Tin foil

- ☐ Trash bags

- ☐ Travel mug

- ☐ Tupperware (If you don't buy tupperware for them, yours will disappear on weekends if they are taking back some of your delicious left overs)

- ☐ Utensils

- ☐

- ☐

Food

- ☐ Bottled water

- ☐ Bread

- ☐ Bulk snacks (candy, granola, dried fruit, etc.)

- ☐ Cereal

- [ ] Coffee or tea (it's going to be a lot cheaper than going to see your neighborhood barista daily unless it is part of their meal plan)
- [ ] Coffee creamer
- [ ] Easy Mac
- [ ] Instant hot chocolate
- [ ] Instant oatmeal or hot cereal
- [ ] Popcorn
- [ ] Ramen
- [ ] Soup
- [ ] Sugar
- [ ]

Clothing

- [ ] Boots (contingent on weather, preference and need)
- [ ] Business-casual clothes (quantity of 1)
- [ ] Coats (spring/winter)
- [ ] Dress shoes (quantity of 1)

- ☐ Hat, gloves, scarf

- ☐ Pajamas

- ☐ Pants/ jeans

- ☐ Underwear

- ☐ Shirts/blouses

- ☐ Slippers

- ☐ Socks

- ☐ Sweats (consider buying a few school spirit wear items in advance in the months to come)

- ☐ Sweaters

- ☐ Swimsuit (quantity of 1)

- ☐

- ☐

Misc.

- ☐ Art materials

- ☐ Beach towel

- ☐ Board games

- ☐ Duct tape

- ☐ Fan

- ☐ Flashlight

- [ ] Lightbulbs

- [ ] Overnight bag

- [ ] Pepper spray (if it's legal in your state)

- [ ] Safety pins

- [ ] Safety whistle

- [ ] Personal keychain alarm

- [ ] Sleep mask

- [ ] Small tool kit

- [ ] Travel bags/travel organizer for toiletries

- [ ] Umbrella

- [ ]

- [ ]

Important Papers

- [ ] Car registration and insurance information

- [ ] Credit card

- [ ] Debit card

- [ ] Driver's license

- [ ] Emergency contact list

- [ ] Financial aid documents

- [ ] Health/dental insurance cards

- [ ] Passport

- [ ] Registration docs

- [ ] Student ID

- [ ]

- [ ]

(College Board, 2016)

CHAPTER 8

Nuggets

This chapter is full of helpful tips and things to consider for college. Some of these tips are good while in college while others are good to prepare for college.

1. Roommates- if you have a preference... try to meet your roommate early... set ground rules for mutual respect. It's going to be important to establish rules that both of you can adhere to. If you have a roommate that is going to have friends over all the time, there has to be a reasonable understanding where you don't end up with an extra person in yours and their space all the time. The space is small as it is and is intended for you and your roommate(s).

2. Pajamas- It is highly likely that you will be woken up in the middle of the night because someone has burned their food. Either they left it unattended or

they just burned it- who knows. I was awoken by the sounds of a fire alarm and had to exit the dorm on more than one occasion in the middle of the night. For this reason, be prepared with pajamas and a robe. Hopefully, you can grab your jacket before having to evacuate until the dorm has been cleared for return. Always evacuate as instructed because you never know if it's a real fire that can be contained or if it's someone burning a grilled cheese in the middle of the night.

3. High school students: Have a minimum 10 weekends spread out over the course of the school year where you try making dinner. If you know how to cook great, if not ask or look it up online. There are instructions to make just about any dish.

4. See if you are able to set a budget. If you are able to work with your parent or guardian, try making a grocery list a few times - see if you can create a list, someone shops the cupboards, someone writes down what's needed, go to the store and do the

shopping with them. Use the list as your reference. Maybe you can hand the cash to the cashier or swipe the debit card.

5. Basic first aid- consider taking a class together as a family or on your own. See if your school offers it first to save money. (Before college or during)

6. <u>Distractions- you have to limit them</u>- you're out on your own. It is not like high school, you need to maintain a certain gpa or you could lose the ability to go to college. Academic probation is a real thing.

7. Don't leave food unattended, fire alarms will wake up everyone in the building.

8. Clean up after yourself. In college, this is a necessity. Be considerate.

9. Lock your door when you leave even when it's just going to the bathroom. There's nothing like coming back to someone in your room or your stuff stolen.

10. How to research using something other than wikipedia or google.- take a trip to the library. You might end up with a paper that requires you to use

sources that are not online. Go to the library. You'll be glad you did.

11. Balance your checkbook on a regular basis.

12. Manage a budget.

13. Learn to use coupons.

14. Finishing Strong- Do not contract **senioritis.** It's when you just want to be done, so you do nothing while in school. Your grades are just as important if not more your senior year, so stick to it and finish strong.

15. Saving (talking budgets with your parents/ guardians, figuring out how to save, etc.)

16. DO NOT OPEN TRANSCRIPTS! In order to get into college, they will require an official final transcript. Request it from your high school or ask them to send it out. Do not open it because once you do, it is no longer considered official. You'll have to request a new one. Let your college open it and be sure to double check with your college to make sure they received it by the deadline.

17. Keeping track of graduation goal in sight. Write it down, track your progress leading up to it. This applies for high school and college.

18. Sure you could eat anything you want now, but should you? Eat healthy as much as possible.

19. Do not schedule any 8 a.m. classes if you are not required to do so unless you are a morning person. It is tough to get to class by 8 a.m. and be ready to learn as a college student. Think how difficult it was in high school. The sweet spot is somewhere around 9:30 a.m. to 10 a.m. Obviously find what works for you, but a lot of students including myself scheduled classes between 9:30 a.m. and 2:30 p.m. and balanced them over the week. There may come a time when this is the only time the class is offered for the year, term and you are required to take it. That is when you would take an 8 a.m. class. Students need to be disciplined regardless of class time. It is so important to get to class on time as

some professors may deduct points from your overall grade for an excess of tardies.

20. Study two hours for every one hour of class per week. For example if you have a one hour class that meets three times a week, you should study six hours for that class during that week. If you can, review your notes the same day as part of your study plan.

- Here's what happens when you go to college... You go to bed when you decide to go to bed. You may be up talking to your friends or your roommate or you might be up late working on homework. Your roommate might be up late working on homework, but steady tapping of the keyboard kept you up half the night. You are now responsible to get up on your own without your parents giving you reminders. Morning seems to come quick. You hit the snooze once, then twice, then a third time. By the time you drag yourself out of bed to dash off to class, you realize that class is on the other side of the campus. You may or may not make it on time. Some professors will count your accumulated tardies as absences after so many. It's always best to go to class anyway, even if you're going to be late.

- Another unwanted scenario is that you could accidentally turn off the snooze and sleep through the class. That's not good either. Did you know that at most colleges, you must attend the first couple of classes or you are automatically withdrawn? What happens if that class was needed to make your status full time? You drop to part time and that for those who are required to be full time may be affected in more ways than one. For some, this may affect their financial aid. For scholarship students, it may affect their aid as well. That's why reading the fine print and asking questions is always important. I cannot count the number of students who go off to college thinking it's going to be a breeze and are rudely awakened right away.

Skipping class in college is not like skipping class in high school. You must maintain an acceptable academic requirement to stay in school. Do yourself a favor, just do your best.

CHAPTER 9

College Planning

One of the best ways to plan for college is to start by strategically planning your high school courses. Set up a meeting with the high school counselor as soon as possible to make sure you are on track for graduation and also that you are in college preparatory classes, meaning you are a college bound student. These are courses that will help strengthen your skills as a student. Colleges will expect you to have a certain level of knowledge before you enroll, so what better way to prepare by taking the courses and learning what they expect you to know before you go to college. If you plan accordingly, you reduce the possibility of having to scramble at the last minute to take a course that you need for graduation and for college entrance.

(ACT, 2017)

Each colleges or universities will have their own specific requirements, be sure to research the criteria for the schools on your wish list. Here is a general list of the typical high school coursework required to get into college. Remember this is nonspecific to any particular school and you need to either contact the school for requirements by reaching out to request information and or go online and look at the enrollment requirements. A typical list of requirements include the following:

Subject	Years/Courses
English	4 years
Math	3 years of Math which usually includes Geometry, Algebra I and Algebra II
Natural Science	2 years (1 Physical, 1 Life) Biology, Chemistry and Physics
Social Sciences	2-3 years (1 US History, 1 World History/Geography/Cultures, Economics, Government)
Fine Arts/ Language	2 years of foreign language (3 years recommended) 1 year (visual arts, music, theater, drama, dance)
Physical Education	2 years
Health	½ year

(ACT, 2017)

By now, you've read through each chapter and have more of an understanding of what to do to plan for college. I reserved this chapter for the end because now you can begin to formulate a plan. Go back and reference chapters as needed. It should all tie together at this point, and you should begin to understand why all of this information is important. It's a lot. Equipping yourself with the tools and knowledge for success will help you in the long run.

It's not too early to start planning for college in the ninth grade. Below is a guide to help you strategize a plan for graduation and college. Read through each one and develop a plan that works for you.

Freshman Year

- Set up an appointment with your counselor to discuss your coursework for college. Make sure they know you are college bound from the beginning. Take the college prep recommended classes. Some may say it's too early to plan... it's not. This doesn't mean that you're in and out of the counselor's office every other day. Check in at the first the first of the year and towards the end of the year. You should have a solid plan for your classes for the year in your first meeting. If you need to meet mid-year because you need assistance preparing for the upcoming term, then by all means meet with your counselor. Meeting towards the later part of the year is for preparing for the upcoming school year. Each school is going to do this differently in terms of how you register. Follow the guidelines for registering with your school. This will more than likely dictate how often you need to meet with the counselor. It's not a bad idea to get a list of graduation requirements to check off the classes taken. Mark the future classes and what term you plan to take them, but don't mark them off until after you have successfully completed the class.

- Set goals for the year. Remember high school is only four years.
- Maintain a solid grades. Do your best.

- Take Advanced Placement (AP) courses and Honors classes when and if you can or plan to register for them the following year.

- Explore colleges (Request information from the schools. Look into tuition costs.)

- Figure out your WHY. (Why are you planning to go to college? What do you want to become as a result of going to college? Why is your education important?)

- Save money for college (If you have a babysitting job, chores or something like that, start to save a portion of that money each time you get paid.)

- Look at extracurricular activities

- Look for volunteer opportunities. College admission is becoming increasingly more competitive. Find ways to help your community and set yourself apart. Many college applications ask about your volunteering efforts. You don't want it to seem as though you started your senior year just to get into college. There are also some

scholarships specific to volunteering. Who knows...
you may find it rewarding.

Sophomore Year

- Meet with your counselor, continue taking recommended classes if possible. Make sure your counselor knows you are still college bound.

- Maintain a solid grades. Do your best.

- Make an academic plan for yourself by setting goals.

- Take the college admissions exam your sophomore year. Many people will disagree with me on this one, but I hold firm to the idea of preparing in advance will help you in the long run. Study for the exam, then take it your sophomore year, so that you can see what subjects you need to improve on. You may be advised against this because you haven't had all of the mathematics on the test. That is true. You will not have had all the math on the test. That's why you take it your sophomore year to get exposure to what's on the test and see what you need to work on. If you need a tutor, this is a perfect way to find out. In addition, why would you put all the pressure on yourself to take the test the first time as a junior, then scramble to take it again as a senior or back to back times as a junior because you didn't do well. If you can afford to take the exam, why not take it to see where they are struggling now so you get the help you need. Have a conversation with your parent or guardian on this and make sure you come to an agreement before registering. You may find that you decide to wait and that's fine if that works for you. I am simply advising you that this is an option that most students aren't even aware is an option for them. Make your decision, but know that this is an option. Note that if you take the official ACT or SAT, take it after you take the PRE ACT or SAT. Consider looking into ACT or SAT bootcamps. Research the cost, benefits and the reputation of the actual camp. Do what is within your affordability range.

- Gather information, schedule and take college tours.(Prepare a list of questions to ask for your tours.)

- If you are in extracurricular activities, continue or explore options.

- Look at scholarship opportunities and apply when applicable. (You do not have to be a senior to apply for some scholarships. Look at the requirements and whenever it is a possibility, go for it. This is why it is important to start searching as early as tenth grade.)

- Check in with the counselor about apprenticeships opportunities, job shadowing and internships.

- Continue to save.

- Make a list of colleges that you'd like to attend. Evaluate, compare and contrast.

- Continue focusing on your WHY. (Your career choice could change and that's ok. Keep focusing though on why your education is important.)

- Continue volunteer efforts.

Junior Year

- Meet with your counselor the first of the year. Get a plan together for the year and make sure you are still on track to graduation and are becoming college ready with each class you take. Talk to your counselor about the schools you are interested in attending.

- Consider AP classes or taking colleges classes in addition to your high school courses. (Taking college classes at a local college could result in you having college classes completed before you enter college. Check with the counselor on the process and requirements. You want to make sure that these classes transfer to your preferred colleges.)

- Maintain solid grades. Do your best. This is typically the toughest year, so put your best foot forward. You can do it!

- Register for the ACT or SAT (Study, take practice exams, get help if you need to before the exam.)

- Start your resume

- Schedule more campus tours for colleges. (Get a list of questions together to ask. If you are close enough to visit some of the schools from the previous year because they are still an option, schedule those as well.)
- Research scholarships, attend scholarship workshops, apply for scholarships if applicable.
- Check in with the counselor about apprenticeship opportunities, job shadowing and internships.
- Continue to volunteer. (Consider volunteering at places that are related to your career interests.)
- Narrow down your school choices. Look at the requirements to apply to each of the possible schools. This is going to be things like college essays, gpa information, classes, etc. Gather that information along with application deadlines and when the applications for the school year open. This is typically early fall of your senior year, so pay attention to dates. Ask for help from parents and/or

your counselor. Perhaps you can create a system that works for you.

- Start scholarship essays over the summer as you are transitioning into senior year if there are any open, apply. Prioritize by deadlines. By now you have been researching and have an idea of the types of scholarships out there. Keep the essays because you may be able to change slightly and recycle accordingly.

- See chapter 6 Financial Aid and Selective Services for more information on financial aid.

- Ask for a transcript at the end of the year to review over the summer. You may also need transcripts for scholarships you are applying to during that time.

- If you have not opened an account and you have enough money saved, open up an account to keep track of your savings. You will need somewhere to keep any scholarship money earned that does not go directly to the school. Decide what type of financial institution and account works best for you. See chapter 6 regarding financial aid disbursements as well.

Senior Year

It's definitely not the time to slow down. Your grades senior year matter just as much as they do freshman year. It can make the difference in some scholarship opportunities, so maintain solid grades both terms. It is more important than ever to finish strong!

Because deadlines really count this year, here's a timeline to help. If you are a procrastinator, now is the time abandon that way of doing things. It's not the time to wait to do what needs to be done. These deadlines will not change (even if there's a technical issue like everyone applying last minute and overloading the system.) You do not want to miss out on applying to your college choices or scholarships because you waited until the last minute and missed a deadline.

Fall (August to November)

- Meet with your school counselor a few times throughout the year starting early on. Make sure you're on track for graduation and to meet your school choices requirements for high school courses. Ask them about district and any scholarships that might be available in your area. Research reputable scholarship sites for additional scholarships.

- Ask teachers and counselors right away for letters of recommendation at the first of the year somewhere around August or September. You will need those for some scholarships and perhaps some college applications. Follow school procedures for requesting letters of recommendations and do not wait. They need time to prepare them. More than likely you are not the only person asking. Help them out by providing them with the resume you worked on during your junior year and notes about you they may not be aware of. This may help them write a solid letter of recommendation.

- Research more scholarships. Use the scholarship worksheet in chapter 6 to keep track of due dates and requirements. Submit before the deadlines.

- Review your ACT or SAT results (Only register if you need to retake it to improve your score. Prepare for it by studying, getting tutoring if necessary and taking practice exams before the exam. Get a good night's sleep the night before and eat breakfast before the exam.)

- Attend a college fair if it's an option.

- Schedule college tours early for any additional schools if applicable, narrow your list of prospective schools down to your final choices.

- Write college essays early August or September. Start applying when the applications open for your anticipated school year. Use the essays you worked on over the summer as references. You may need to change them to fit the essay question, but this is a great place to start. Each school will have its own deadline. Make a list of the choices and write on your calendar their application due dates. Try to get them in no later than one week before they are due to avoid any errors. Mark them off once you have submitted your application and have received your confirmation emails. Recycle essays as needed and customize to fit essay requirements. Follow the application guidelines for admissions. Work with your counselor on this and your parent or guardian.

- Ask for official transcripts in advance for scholarships. You will need one transcript for yourself, so that you can enter information online for scholarships. Ask the office for official transcripts early (ask for around 4 to start) for scholarships that need to be sent out via mail. Those should be sealed and not opened. A transcript that is opened is considered unofficial and you will have to resend a new one. Save yourself a step and keep them sealed. Timeframe to ask for these should be around the end of August if your school is in already in session in August. If your school starts in September, then ask for these mid September. Asking the first week of school is difficult on the office staff because there is so much to do at the start of the school year. The other option is to ask for these over the summer before school starts... just not the week before school. That too is a busy time preparing for students to return. Remember that these transcripts are for scholarships that you are applying for. You will be requesting the school send official transcripts to colleges after you submit admission applications.

- Decide if you are going to gather your items throughout the school year or towards the end of the year. Reference the checklist as an example of possible items needed in chapter 7.

- Figure out how you want to acquire items needed for school. For example, I started in August buying an extra item when I did my regular shopping (like shampoo, toothpaste, a towel and washcloth) until January when I completed my list of items needed. My student also knew though what school they were headed to by then which made it was easier to plan out what to buy each pay period. I wanted to avoid spending an astronomical amount over the summer. I used the current sales promotions at that time to buy the printer and refrigerator.

- Continue volunteering.

Winter (December to February)

- If your school has interview or audition processes, be sure to schedule and wrap these up during this time if possible.

- Start and finish your FAFSA. (Free Application for Federal Student Aid) Remember this is free. If you are applying for this and you have to pay, you are on the wrong website. Check with the school or counselor for the accurate site. See chapter 6 for further details.

- Request your high school to send official transcripts be sent to each college or university you applied to. Remember that colleges and universities will require an official transcript at the end of the year as well to make sure you have successfully completed your last term, so keep your grades up.

- Schedule time to meet with your counselor to make sure each school has everything requested for admission. This will include transcripts, letter of recommendations, test results. You can send the ACT or SAT to each school, but you need to confirm that it is done. Your counselor should be able to help you check things off your list regarding this.

- If you have not received confirmation that your application has been received by each school, follow up by phone or email.

- Continue to apply for scholarships. Look at any scholarships available at your choice colleges to see if they have them. Most will have some scholarships available for submission. Apply to any and all that apply to you. There may be essays. If this is the case, reference the ones you're using and adjust accordingly to fit essay requirements.

- Check the email the school has assigned to you at least twice a week for any updates or things they need from you (That is if they assign one during this process). This is typically how they might communicate. Check your other emails as well, but make sure this is top of mind every week. You don't want to miss any deadlines.

Spring (March to June)

- You will begin to receive letters in the mail with decision results from each school. Make your decision on which school you will attend. Talk it over with your parents or guardian and your counselor. Follow the steps to accept admission to your school choice right away. Often times, there will be a checklist for you. Use it to stay on track with what needs to be done.

- Apply for housing as soon as the application is available if you are staying on campus. This is typically somewhere around March or April, but check with your chosen school because it may vary. Don't be afraid to call the school anytime you have questions about things like this.

- Since you have applied for financial aid in the winter, you should be able to see what type of aid you might be eligible for. Make your budget decisions after you have this information. You can't really figure out budget necessities without knowing what type of aid you will have.

- Just before graduation, request your final transcript be sent to your chosen school. Make sure you follow up with your college or university to confirm it has been received. Some schools will not have transcripts ready until just after school is out for the summer. You will need to call or visit the high school if it has not been sent out. Colleges are very firm on receiving them by a certain time. Your enrollment can literally be cancelled if they do not receive it by the deadline or if it does not have the correct postmark date. Another important note is to not open an official transcript that is being sent out to a college. If you are taking it to the school, take it sealed. The moment you open it even if it is in the presence of that department, it is considered unofficial and you will have to acquire a new official one. Trust me on this, I speak from experience. Years ago, the registrar watched me open my official transcript and hand it to her, then declared it unofficial a week later.

- Make sure you've done everything required for graduation.

- Plan for any AP exams or college finals if you are taking college classes while attending high school. Check out websites that offer free AP practice exams. Take them as many times as you want if they are free. Make sure of course they are legitimate websites. Check in with your AP teacher for details on this and other support out there to prepare. If you are getting additional help to plan for the exams, continue to get that support. Study well in advance. If there are fees for the AP exams, make sure you sign up and pay by the deadline.

- Secure your summer job. Continue to save.
- If you do not acquire your items little by little over the school year, use the checklist in chapter seven to start buying what you need.

(Campus Explorer, 2017) (ACT, 2017)

I hope this book has been as insightful for you as it was for me writing it. Revisit the chapters in this book as many times as you need. It's a lot of information, but you've got this. Now you have a guide and a greater understanding of what you need to do. It's time to get to work. Each of you reading this book are at different stages. Don't compare yourself to others who are ahead of you or behind. Focus on you and what you need to do to get what you need done.

In this book, *Life Skills & College Planning Made Easy: Everything a Teen Needs to Know*, I've done my best to incorporate the things that are good to know, should know and need to know. I did a lot of the research to make sure that I was sending a knowledgeable, well informed student on their way to higher education. I want you to be confident and cultivated in financial literacy, so that you can make good decisions for yourself that benefit you later in life. The skills that are mentioned in this book are tools to guide you on your quest.

I have had an abundance of experience with high school students as well as adults who were returning to school. The overwhelming response from a large majority of the adults was that they wished they knew then what I was showing them now. In other words, they missed out on a lot and most of them felt unprepared for college regardless of whether or not it was their first time attending or reentering. That's why so many of them were returning to school. It didn't work out the first time. Either way, it was a pleasure to guide them through the process and now I am excited to equip you with the knowledge necessary to get you started.

Though the timeline in the last chapter spans through the school year, you should be applying for scholarships on into the summer if they are available. There are some scholarships specifically for college students, so don't stop searching. Search high and low and try to start on the things you need to do as soon as you can.

If you've ever heard the phrase the early bird gets the worm, you'll see how this applies to you as you prepare for college. It's going to be up to you to get the worm. You will need to be willing to put in the work. If you wait around and get things done last minute, you run the risk of missing deadlines or producing less than stellar work. You are an adult now or very close to it, and the reality is that it's time to step it up. You're going to college! You've made it this far and you have the potential to do so much more. It will require focus on your part. A team like family and friends are always helpful, but the reality is that not everyone has the support. I know that some of you may not have the help and you may need to do this alone. Check in with your counselor and see if they can help. Just don't give up.

It's not going to easy, but that does not mean you can't do it. It just means it will be a little tougher and organization will be your friend. I can't promise you that everything will go according to plan, but I can say that if you don't try, you will never know what could have been. I wish you all the best on your journey. Thank you for taking the time to read this book. I truly hope it has been helpful. Good luck!!!

Written By: Patrice Torrez ©
Cover by Hector Curriel ©Patrice Torrez 2017
BeBe Abner
2017 ISBN: 978-0-9993771-0-9

Bibliography

ACT.(2017). *College Planning.* (ACT, Inc.)

Retrieved from

http://www.act.org/content/act/en/product

s-and-services/act-profile/college-

planning.html

Campus Explorer. (2017). *High School Senior*

Timeline and Checklist. Retrieved

from Campus Explorer:

http://www.campusexplorer.com/college-

advice-tips/6BCDBA67/High-School-Senior-

Timeline-and-Checklist/

College Board. (2016). *Big Future.* (T. C. Board,

Producer) Retrieved from

https://bigfuture.collegeboard.org/get-

in/making-a-decision/off-to-college-

checklist: www.collegeboard.org

Council For Economic Education. (2016, January). *Survey of States Economic and Personal Finance In Our Nation's Schools 2016.* Retrieved December 30, 2016, from http://councilforeconed.org: http://councilforeconed.org/wp/wp-content/uploads/2016/02/sos-16-final.pdf

Council for Higher Education Accreditation. (2017, April 3). *Information About Accreditation.* Retrieved June 29, 2017, from www.chea.org: http://www.chea.org/4DCGI/cms/review.html?Action=CMS_Document&DocID=48&MenuKey=main

Niz, E. S. (2016). *12 Basic Life Skills Every Kid Should Know by High School.* (Meredith's Corporation) Retrieved from www.parenting.com: http://www.parenting.com/child/child-

development/12-basic-life-skills-every-kid-
should-know-high-school

Soukup, R. (n.d.). *48 Life Skills Everyone Should
Learn*. Retrieved from
www.livingwellspendingless.com:
http://www.livingwellspendingless.com/201
6/01/08/48-life-skills-everyone-learn/

Acknowledgements

To my husband, thank you for pushing me to excel. Your support drives me towards excellence.

To my wonderful children, you are the reason why I do what I do. So proud of the people you have become.

To Samilya Z and Dave Lee SCRW, you two have been the epitome of excellent friends and encouragers. Your constant push helped me see this project through to fruition. All the text messages and emails to check in and hold me accountable paid off. Sam, your consistency during a time when things seemed to be so hectic was so refreshing. This experience was a personal one because I was going through the process as I wrote this book. Experience has made me a better teacher. Thank you.

To Professor Bok, thank you for the gentle nudges and suggestions that there might just be something magnificent within. Thank you also for leading by example. Without your encouragement, I might not have ever written a word in book form.

To my kids at FAIR School Downtown, I am so incredibly proud of you. There are so many of you. You all are so wonderful and you know who you are. I am so fortunate to have gotten to know you and watch you grow. Grab a piece of the universe and imprint your name on the stars.

To Hilary, I am so thankful for you- we both are. You found a way to make this process easier. You gave us the tools needed to start our journey. The real journey of a hero begins with a call to action. The sign of a real hero is when they answer the call. I kind of feel like that's what you did. Thank you.

To my family from afar, thank you for always encouraging me to keep going and believing in me. I love you guys!

CJW, your unwavering support means so much to me. Thank you.

To Mabel, this one is for you. Pale Blue.